René Burri
Cuba y Cuba

Text by Marco Meier
Poetry by Miguel Barnet

Smithsonian Institution Press
Washington, D.C.

Published 1998 in the United States of America
by Smithsonian Institution Press
in association with Federico Motta Editore, Milan

Translation from Italian and Spanish by Renata Treitel

Library of Congress Cataloging-in-Publication Data

Burri, René
   [Cuba y Cuba. English]
   Cuba y Cuba / René Burri : text by Marco Meier : poetry
by Miguel Barnet.
       p. cm.
   Originally published in Italian in 1994 by Federico Motta
Editore of Milan
   ISBN 1-56098-781-2 (alk. paper)
   1. Cuba—Pictorial works.   2. Cuba—Description and
travel.   3. Cuba—Poetry.   I. Meier, Marco.   II. Barnet,
Miguel, 1940–   .   III. Title.
   F1765.3.88713   1998
   972.91—dc21   97-43813
                                              CIP
                                              r97

04 03 02 01 00 99 98   5 4 3 2 1

Printed by Arti Grafiche Motta, Milan
Manufactured in Italy, not at government expense

Contents

Photographs 1984–1993

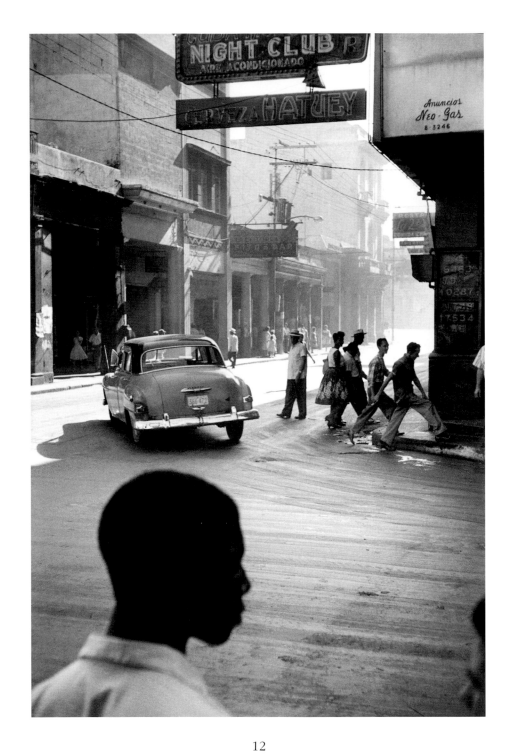

Hope in Times of Crisis

Marco Meier

The lack of balanced tones in all judgments on Cuba is disturbing, no matter where they come from. The world does not want to hear of socialism anymore. Europe got rid of its own socialism efficiently. The ideological dwindling does not interest any one. Once and for all, people look in other directions. The last socialistic systems are being observed with curiosity. And in the world community, the game of the free market is happily played out and soon people will find themselves in trouble. Capitalism can founder in merry solitude and with total peace of mind. It is an understandable logic when it is about the defunct models of Eastern European stamp. Very soon this type of real socialism will not be missed by anyone. But there is still the problem of Cuba.

In the seventies and the eighties, when we Western intellectuals slowly realized that the examples of Eastern European socialism were not perfectly successful and that, without Mao, China too would lose its power of attraction, the Caribbean represented a transforming trend in which many people put their hope. Later on, at one point, there was also Nicaragua. After all, this southern offshoot of the New World joined our social revolutionary imaginings in an explosive mixture with the fantastic world of magic realism. Latin American dictators, generals, and *caudillos* represented simultaneously the most hated and the most admired role models of political man on the world stage of socialism.

But suddenly the scene has changed. Fidel does not smoke *cohibas* anymore, he welcomes Benetton to Havana, and gives the dollar free rate of exchange. On the thirty-fifth year of the revolution, extreme poverty rules. Everything is in crisis. For years the trip from Havana's José Martí airport has taken place on a very wide, but poorly lit, highway. The sparse street lamps still functioning proclaim that here a very dark night prevails. But the taxi driver has long been accustomed to this and speeds along like lightning. Twice he swerves abruptly and informs us that he has barely missed two cyclists who were weaving in and out of traffic.

Bicycles built in China lack lights, and only the deluxe models are provided, at best, with a bell. But, under the robust legs of the Cubans, these steel nags become nimble vehicles that consent to an almost unlimited freedom. And those who have experienced speed once will never be willing to slow down.

For the tourists too, the crisis makes itself felt slowly. In the last few weeks at the Hotel Inglaterra, the generous, *à discretion* breakfast buffet has disappeared. Today the guests must purchase their own coupons on a daily basis and, furthermore, must fight to get sufficient helpings of coffee, sweets, and fruit. A second cup of coffee is never served without a surcharge. And bread literally has disappeared from the tables. Those who still lodge at the aristocratic Nacional, the most prestigious hotel in the New World, know nothing of these rationings. In one word, for foreigners the crisis is relative.

But for the Cubans it is total. Humiliated, Raúl, a photographer with official status and a deeply, committed supporter of the Cuban revolution, lets slip out: *"Hay hambre,* there is hunger," he whispers, "even in my family," which for him has been simply unthinkable of his beloved Cuba of the last thirty years. Even the minimal rations that the state guarantees and that are delivered on presentation of the *libreta* (coffee, sugar, beans, rice, oil, and bread) have been partially reduced to one-half. Often it is impossible to get rations at all. For Raúl to talk about hunger is like betraying the revolution. It was the pride of every Cuban and, for this very reason, Fidel Castro has remained in power as commander-in-chief, despite the latent, growing restlessness: hunger, a daily reality for millions of human beings in almost all of the Latin American countries, was no longer possible in Cuba after dictator Batista's times.

"Cuba is living a tragedy in the original sense: a drama without solution taking us to an inexorably woeful end. What is against nature is that Cubans don't speak up." Thus Jesús Díaz, a Cuban writer now living in Berlin, writes in an essay: "Actually, all those who know today's Cuba are unanimous in stating that a call for change moves across the island. But it is expressed in the form of a nerve-racking silence, of a terrible calm."

The drama described by Díaz is undoubtedly in progress, the call for change cannot be not heard. But even five years ago, things here were no different. And ten, fifteen years ago, some discerning minds had already warned that, sooner or later, the unilateral financial dependence on the ex-Soviet Union would take Cuba toward a catastrophe. In this late fall weekend in Havana, there is an unreal calm, an exceptional atmosphere of a particular kind, a tension, even a great sense of expectation. And over it all, there hangs a heat that is abnormal, even for Cuba: 39 degrees Celsius in the shade, tropical humidity. All of Havana is exhausted. No cars move along the streets. There is a purposeless bustle, a soothingly calm sea; from time to time a bus; on the streets there seem to be only couples in love strolling as if in a dream and dragging themselves placidly along or slowly pedaling their bicycle in seemingly self-forgetfulness. As far as the eye can see, bicycles: usually loaded with four or more persons acrobatically piled up, true traveling embraces, muscular behinds in sheer stretch tights and under a tank top, firm breasts, strong, tanned backs. And all of this fantastically twined, shiny, slippery, sparkling. It is not easy to understand who is resting and who is pedaling. One is the offshoot of the other, a blaze of despair in movement, joyful ghosts in the city. A people that dares. Cuba is waiting.

Unlike what we had always felt on this island, this calm does not strike us as terrifying, the silence has not shaken our nerves. Despite poverty and the imminent catastrophe, there throbs the rhythm of a new hope under the cover of a loathed discipline; there seems to be an aroused Caribbean pride behind the collective silence.

Was it a last-minute prank or the grumbling indifference of a people turned childish under socialism? Or perhaps was it we Europeans, carried away in the intensity of the southern tropics, to imagine a new socialistic romanticism? Were we also sick with that "Castro-enteritis," defined and criticized by the writer Guillermo Cabrera Infante, for the last 28 years in exile in London, which would induce the "poorly informed foreigners" into still believing in Fidel Castro's great exploits? In short, would any projection be utopian and hopeless, would no model of a just society survive on this Caribbean island? Perhaps as a commemorative monument. And, indeed, the world has not become more just in these last few years.

This look at Cuba lends itself to other reflections as well, in spite of the contemptuous ideological mentality of the West. Or maybe just because of it. In any event, "To speak of Cuba, it is necessary to start from a fundamental premise: good will," writes the Uruguayan writer Eduardo Galeano. From the first days of the revolution, one of the few who has lived his encounter with Cuba with fidelity, enthusiasm, and respect, is the photographer René Burri. In his thirty-plus-year-old analysis of the revolutionary model, the constant of a proud Cuban people has remained untouched. This encounter is the result of a reciprocal acknowledgment. The Cuba seen by Burri has a future.

Perhaps the real cultural revolution on the Caribbean island started only with the present crisis. For the first time in more than five hundred years, Cuba is free from any dependence on a colonial power. It is a specific characteristic of Cuban history that, after each victory over a colonial power, this country repeatedly ended up depending on another power. The free world could see that this does not happen again. In its history, after each political and economic collapse, Cuba has always recovered with unusual rapidity. There is no lack of material for this country to recover on its own: sugar, nickel, oil, tobacco, tourism, and biotechnology. Why couldn't the tiny Cuban state be able to succeed pragmatically in exploiting the opportunities offered by the world market in order to strengthen its own economy and then devote itself more intensively to its own specific model of a just world? Young politicians like Roberto Rebaina, Minister of Foreign Affairs, Carlos Lage, Minister of Economy, Ricardo Alarcón, president of the House of Representatives, or Abel E. Prieto, president of the Writers' and Artists' Association, seem to agree on this point: world economic interdependence is a fact that cannot be overlooked, but economic liberalism and capitalism are ideologies not to be accepted without criticism.

However, according to the most recent news, Fidel Castro has already suppressed the first stirrings of a private economy at birth. The florists that have been appearing fleetingly in greater numbers lately on Havana's streets, have disappeared again. A bad omen? The ex-"court photographer," Alberto Korda, feels gloomy and without illusions: "With Fidel, change is impossible. For a time we called him "big foot," because he did not know how to dance and kept stepping on his partners' toes." In Cuba, a *líder* without a musical ear sooner or later takes a false step. *Trabajo sí, rumba no.* It would be the death of the Cuban *alma*.

Text and poetry translated from the Italian and Spanish by Renata Treitel

27

Revolution

Between you and me
there's a pile of contradictions
which flock together to make
me the startled one
beads on his brow
and he builds you up.

                    Miguel Barnet

You made me suffer. But I grew inside. And you were the very one who freed me from those thorns that hurt me so deeply.
What would life mean without you? Why do we speak of communism, political parties? Let us talk of the blue house, of the patio with gigantic leaves, of clean, free, musical hospitals.

Let us talk of the "special period," the permanent emergency we Cubans have lived, the daily tension, the rebuilding of the spirit, the daily decency. Of the solid mortar of which the cane cropper is made, the sensuousness of the generous hips perfumed with musk, these eyes that no longer avoid the other's glance, but that, on the contrary, look for it, pin it, challenge it. What to say then to the one who asks me why I live in Cuba? I have no answer. [M. B.]

33

Vedado

On your streets of thick trees and shadows,
under your summer sky,
blue and unique,
in your oozing parks, mythological,
is the outline of my life.
I covet your light clear
like lightning.
I go toward your lonely poplars.
Exultant I look for the wary
noon ants.
I want to stay awake in you.
Live inside what I love,
like in music whose soil is mine.

Miguel Barnet

Vedado is a neighborhood in Havana. The navel of the world. The not-to-be missed tour of every traveler. I know of no other neighborhood that is so beautiful, with its chipped houses, its stray dogs, its ancestral narrow streets of rough stones and that perpendicular sun that splits the cement of its sidewalks. Vedado is the vortex around which the country turns. Now it is invaded by tourists from the north or by the Olmec [Mexicans]. No matter. The vendor of essences keeps piping among the leaves to make the hummingbird fall asleep on the terraces. Vedado is an indescribable feast. [M. B.]

DATE DUE

OCT 2 5 2006	